The BUMPER BOOK OF very SILLY JOKES

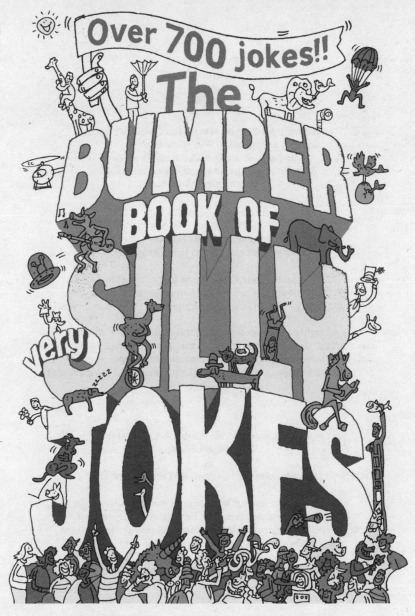

Over 700 jokes!!

The BUMPER BOOK OF very SILLY JOKES

Illustrated by Jane Eccles

MACMILLAN CHILDREN'S BOOKS

First published 2013 by Macmillan Children's Books
an imprint of Pan Macmillan
20 New Wharf Road, London N1 9RR
Associated companies throughout the world
www.panmacmillan.com

ISBN 978-1-4472-2613-0

20

A CIP catalogue record for this book is available from
the British Library.

Printed and bound by CPI Group (UK) Ltd, Croydon CR0 4YY

To all my friends who have been so kind
and encouraging, and mean the world
to me (they know who they are),
to my Graham who has been a total star
and with special thanks to Tricia. (JE)

Contents

Animals 1

Birthdays 18

Bizarre Books 24

Body Bits 26

Brainteasers 30

Bugs 40

Dinosaurs 46

Doctor, Doctor! 52

Family Fun 61

Favourite Characters 73

Food 79

Geography 98

Ghosts 104

Gross! 116

History 120

Holiday Time 130

Jobs 146

Knock, Knock — 163

Love — 171

Magic — 173

Monsters — 178

Music — 188

Nature — 193

Pirates — 200

School — 202

Science and Technology — 218

Silly Signs — 224

Space — 227

Sport — 234

Vampires — 242

Waiter! — 251

Weather — 256

What do you call . . . — 261

Animals

Why do cows lie down when it's cold?
To keep each udder warm.

**What do you get if
you cross a kangaroo
with a sheep?**
A woolly jumper.

**What did the mouse say
when it broke its front teeth?**
Hard cheese.

**What do you get
when you cross a cat
with a lemon?**
A sour puss.

**What's the difference between an
elephant and a biscuit?**
You can't dunk an elephant in your tea.

**What's black, white and
red all over?**
A blushing zebra.

What kind of fish can't swim?
Dead ones.

How do you communicate with a fish?
Drop him a line.

Why did the chicken join a band?
Because he had a fantastic pair of drumsticks.

Why did the blackbird fly into the library?
It was looking for bookworms.

When does a duck get up?
At the quack of dawn.

How does an elephant get down from a tree?
He sits on a leaf and waits till autumn.

Two tigers were walking down the high street. One of them says to the other, 'Quiet for a Saturday night, isn't it?'

What kind of cats love water?
Octopusses.

Why do horses look sad?
Because they have long faces.

Why can't a leopard hide?
Because he's always spotted.

What do you get if you pour boiling water down a rabbit hole?
Hot cross bunnies.

What do you do with a blue whale?
Try to cheer it up.

What do cats eat for breakfast?
Mice Krispies.

Why is it hard to bury an elephant?
Because it's an enormous undertaking.

What's the wettest animal in the world?
A reindeer.

**How do horses
propose?**
On bended neigh.

What do you call a three-legged donkey?
A wonky.

What kind of key opens a banana?
A monkey.

Where does a chicken go when it dies?
To oven.

Where do sheep go for their haircuts?
The baa baa shop.

What's a rabbit's favourite kind of music?
Hip hop.

Why did the pony cough?
He was a little hoarse.

What's a shark's favourite game?
Bite and seek.

Why is a puppy good at DIY?
*Because it's always doing little
jobs around the house.*

**Mike: Would you like to play with our new
dog?**
*Joanne: I'm not sure. He looks very fierce. Does
he bite?*
Mike: That's what I want to find out.

What do you call a frog with no hind legs?
Unhoppy.

Which cat purrs more than any other?
A purrsian cat.

**What do you get if you cross
a skunk with an owl?**
*Something that smells, but
doesn't give a hoot.*

Why is it difficult to have a conversation with a goat?
It always butts in.

Why won't banks allow kangaroos to open accounts?
Their cheques always bounce.

What do you get if you cross a dog with a telephone?
A golden receiver.

What do you get from a clever oyster?
Pearls of wisdom.

**What do you call a pig
that knows karate?**
A pork chop.

**Why are giraffes slow to
apologize?**
*It takes them a very long time to
swallow their pride.*

**What's black and white
and eats like a horse?**
A zebra.

**What's black and white and
makes loads of noise?**
A zebra with a drum kit.

**Why did the owl
say, 'Tweet,
tweet'?**
*Because she didn't
give a hoot.*

Why were the elephants thrown out of the swimming pool?
Because they couldn't keep their trunks up.

What's a crocodile's favourite game?
Snap.

**What do you get if you
cross a chicken with a dog?**
Pooched eggs.

What bird is always out of breath?
A puffin.

Birthdays

What do you get every birthday?

A year older.

**What did the big candle say
to the little candle?**

You're too young to go out.

**Sam: Well, I guess my birthday
wish didn't come true.**
Amanda: How do you know?
Sam: You're still here.

**Steve: Why didn't you give me
anything for my birthday?**
Kate: You told me to surprise you.

Was anybody famous born on your birthday?
No, only babies were born on my birthday.

Why do we put candles on top of birthday cakes?
Because it would be too hard to put them on the bottom.

How can you tell that birthdays are good for you?
Because statistics show that the people who have the most birthdays live the longest.

John: I get heartburn every time I eat birthday cake.
Mike: Take the candles off next time.

What's the best kind of birthday present?
Another one.

Dan: Did you go to Katherine's birthday party?
James: No, the invite said 'four to eight' and I'm nine.

Matt: When's your birthday?
Becky: 5 August.
Matt: Which year?
Becky: Every year!

What do you call an adult balloon?

A blown-up.

Bizarre Books

Cruising in the Arctic Ocean by I.C. King

The Basics of Food
by Brendan Butter

The Art of Breakfast by Chris P. Bacon

Missing You Already by Miles Apart

A Dog's Life by Norah Bone

The Worst Journey in the World by Hellen Back

Potty Training by Enid A. Wee

Life on the Ocean Waves by Eva Lot

Privacy in the Home
by Annette Curtain

Get Rich Quick by Robin Banks

A Continental Breakfast by Roland Jam

Body Bits

What did one ear say to the other ear?
Between us we have brains!

**How do you stop a cold
going to your chest?**
Tie a knot in your neck.

**What should you do if you
split your sides laughing?**
Run until you get a stitch.

**What should you do if
your nose goes on strike?**
Picket.

**What do you get if someone hits
you on the head with an axe?**
A splitting headache.

**What happened when the
two red blood cells fell in love?**
They loved in vein.

**What kind of bandages
do people wear after
heart surgery?**
Ticker tape.

How do you cure dandruff?
Cut off your head.

Kate: Do you ever file your nails?
*Karen: Eew! No, I throw them
away immediately!*

Mark: I've just swallowed a bone.
Simon: Are you choking?
Mark: No, I'm serious!

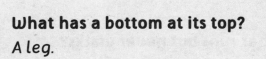

What has a bottom at its top?
A leg.

How long can you live without a brain?
Well, how old are you?

Brain-teasers

What runs but never walks?
Water.

**What's black when it's clean
and white when it's dirty?**
A blackboard.

What gets bigger the more you take away?
A hole

How many months of the year have twenty-eight days?
All of them.

What can you serve but not eat?
A volleyball.

What is full of holes but can still hold water?
A sponge.

What has a head and a tail but no body?
A coin.

What has arms and legs but no head?
A chair.

What goes up but never comes down?
Your age.

What nut has no shell?
A doughnut.

**What goes up and down
but doesn't move?**
The temperature.

 **What can you hold without touching it?**
Your breath.

What runs around a field without moving?
A fence.

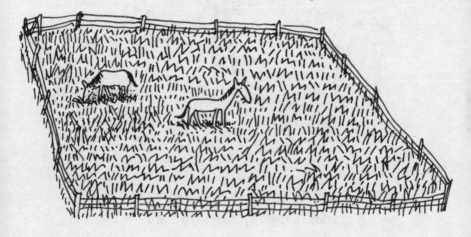

**What has one head,
one foot but four legs?**
A bed.

What's yours, but others use it more than you do?
Your name.

What's pointed in one direction but headed in the other?
A pin.

**What needs to be answered,
but doesn't ask a question?**
A telephone.

**What do you
get after it's
been taken?**
Your photo.

**What can you make
that can't be seen?**
A noise.

What has four legs but can't walk?
A table.

What ring is square?
A boxing ring.

What can you keep but give away at the same time?
A cold.

**What gets wetter
the more it dries?**
A towel.

**What room has no floors,
no walls and no windows?**
A mushroom.

What runs but has no legs?
A tap.

Bugs

Where do bees go to the toilet?
At the BP station.

**What insect runs away
from everything?**
A flea.

**Why do millipedes taste
like chewing gum?**
They're wrigglies.

What do you call a fly with no wings?
A walk.

What kind of bugs live in clocks?
Ticks.

Who's a wasp's favourite singer?
Sting.

What is a snail?
A slug wearing a crash helmet.

What does a caterpillar do on the first of January?
Turns over a new leaf.

What did the big sister bug say to the younger brother bug?
Stop bugging me!

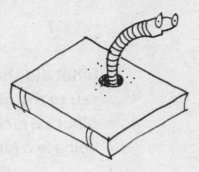

**What did the bookworm
say to the librarian?**
May I burrow this book?

Why was the bee's hair sticky?
Because she used a honeycomb.

What did the firefly say to her best friend?
You glow, girl!

**What did the boy maggot
say to the girl maggot?**
*What's a nice girl like you
doing in a joint like this?*

Why do bees hum?
Because they don't know the words.

What do you call a bee born in May?
A maybe.

Why was the glow worm confused?
She didn't know whether she was coming or glowing.

Why did the bees go on strike?
Because they wanted more honey and shorter working flowers.

Why don't centipedes play football?
By the time they've laced up all their boots, the match would be over.

Dinosaurs

What do you call a blind dinosaur?
A doyouthinkhesawus.

What does a T-rex eat?
Anything it wants!

Why did the dinosaur go on a diet?
He was too big for his scales.

**What do you call a dinosaur
wearing tight shoes?**
My-foot-is-saurus.

**What does a dinosaur get
from scrubbing floors?**
Dino-sores.

Why did the dinosaur take a bath?
To get ex-stinked.

**What do you get when
a dinosaur sneezes?**
Out of the way!

Why did the dinosaur cross the road?
Because the chicken hadn't evolved yet.

**What do you call a dinosaur
that won't stop talking?**
A dinobore.

Why do dinosaurs eat raw meat?
*Because they don't know
how to cook.*

What followed the dinosaurs?
Their tails.

What has a spiked tail, armour plates and sixteen wheels?

A stegosaurus on roller skates.

How did dinosaurs pass their exams?
With extinction.

Why are there old dinosaur bones in the museum?
Because they can't afford to buy new ones.

How does a T-rex greet you?
Pleased to eat you.

Which is the scariest dinosaur?
The terrordactyl.

Doctor, Doctor!

Doctor, Doctor, I think I'm invisible.

I'm sorry, I can't see you now.

Doctor, Doctor, I've swallowed a clock!
There's no cause for alarm.

Doctor, Doctor, you've got to help me out!
Certainly, which way did you come in?

Doctor, Doctor, I feel like a guitar.
Sit down while I make some notes.

Doctor, Doctor, I feel like a needle.
Yes, I can see your point.

**Doctor, Doctor, I think I've been
bitten by a vampire!**
Drink this glass of water.
Will that cure me?
*No, but we'll be able to see
if your neck is leaking.*

**Doctor, Doctor, I feel
like a canary.**
*I can't tweet you,
go and see a vet.*

Doctor, Doctor, I keep thinking I'm a goat.
How long has this been going on?
Ever since I was a kid.

Doctor, Doctor, I think I need glasses.
You certainly do, this is the library!

**Doctor, Doctor, I feel like
a pack of cards.**
I'll deal with you later.

Doctor, Doctor, I feel like a dog.
Sit!

Doctor, Doctor, can I get a second opinion?
Absolutely – come back again tomorrow.

Doctor, Doctor, I keep losing my memory.
When did you first notice that?
When did I first notice what?

Doctor, Doctor, everybody ignores me.
Next!

Doctor, Doctor, I only have fifty seconds to live!
Hang on, I'll be with you in a minute.

Doctor, Doctor, I smell like a fish.
Oh, you poor sole.

Doctor, Doctor, I think I'm a spoon.
Sit over there, and don't stir.

Doctor, Doctor, do you have a cure for sleepwalking?
Sprinkle drawing pins on your bedroom floor before you go to sleep.

Doctor, Doctor, I feel like an apple.
We must get to the core of this.

Doctor, Doctor, I have a terrible pain in my lower back.
We must get to the bottom of this.

Doctor, Doctor, I feel like a pair of curtains.
Pull yourself together!

Doctor, Doctor, I've swallowed a dictionary!
Shh! Don't breathe a word to anybody.

**Doctor, Doctor,
I feel like a wasp.**
Buzz off!

Doctor, Doctor, I feel like a piano.
Sit down while I make some notes.

Family Fun

Mum: It was nice of you to let your little brother have the first go on your new skates.

Daughter: I wanted to know if the ice on the lake was thick enough.

Dad: Didn't you hear me calling you?
Son: Yeah, but you told me not to answer you back.

What do you call two people who embarrass you in front of your friends?
Mum and Dad.

Sarah: My nan was a medium.
Laura: Really? Mine was an extra large.

Little brother: I think I've got an inferiority complex.
Big sister: Rubbish – you ARE inferior!

What's a baby's motto?
If at first you don't succeed,
cry, cry, cry again.

Mum: Did you take a bath?
Son: Why, is there one missing?

Dad: Who broke the window?
Mark: It was Andy, Dad. He ducked
when I threw a stone at him.

**Dad: Would you like any
help with your homework?**
James: No, thanks. I'd rather
get it wrong on my own.

Big sister: I can marry anyone I please.
Little brother: But you don't please anyone.

Why are grandpa's teeth like the stars?
Because they come out at night.

Little sister: Can you help me with my maths homework?
Big brother: No. It wouldn't be right.
Little sister: I know, but you could at least try.

Dad: Don't eat off your knife.
Jake: But my fork leaks!

Julie: How old are you?

Mum: I'm forty-five. But I don't look it, do I?

Julie: No, but you used to.

Why does grandma cover her mouth with her hand when she sneezes?

To catch her false teeth.

Laura: The rubbish bin must be full of toadstools.
Mum: What?
Laura: There's not mushroom.

Sam: You're wearing my school jumper!
Rachel: No, I'm not. Yours is the one I dropped in the river.

Luke: Mum, I feel sick as a dog.

Mum: OK, I'll call the vet.

Dad: Why are you eating so fast?

James: I don't want to lose my appetite.

Neil: Mum, you know that vase that's been handed down from generation to generation?

Mum: Yes?

Neil: Well, this generation's dropped it.

Charlotte: Mum, do you think I should take up the piano as a career?

Mum: No, I think you should put the lid down as a favour.

Dad: Didn't you hear me hammering on your bedroom door last night, Alice?

Alice: Don't worry, Dad, I was playing my music really loudly so you didn't disturb me.

Helen: I hear your brother is very interested in energy conservation.

Laura: Yes, he conserves all the energy he possibly can!

Mum: Why is your sister crying, Lily?

Lily: Because I wouldn't let her have one of my crisps.

Mum: Well, what did she do with her crisps?

Lily: She cried when I ate those too.

Steph: Mum, you know you're constantly worrying that I'll fail maths?

Mum: Yes?

Steph: Well, your worries are over.

Mrs Woods: After a few years of being married, we heard the patter of tiny feet.
Mrs Bennett: Was it a boy or a girl?
Mrs Woods: Neither, it was rats.

Mum caught William with the cake tin. 'And what do you think you're up to?' she asked.
'I'm up to my sixth scone,' he replied.

Favourite Characters

What do you call James Bond in the bath?
Bubble 07.

What's a superhero's favourite part of the joke?
The punch line.

What do you get if Batman and Robin get squashed by a steamroller?
Flatman and Ribbon.

Why didn't Superman know he could fly?

He didn't know his cape-abilities.

What's large, green and sits in the corner on its own all day?

The Incredible Sulk.

How does Batman's mum call him for dinner?
Dinner dinner dinner dinner BATMAN!

**Why does Batman
wear his pants
outside his trousers?**
To keep them clean.

Where is Spiderman's homepage?
On the world wide web.

Why was Cinderella thrown off the rounders team?
Because she ran away from the ball.

Why would Snow White make a good judge?
Because she's the fairest one of all.

What was Dr Jekyll's favourite game?
Hyde and seek.

Why was Tigger peering into the toilet?
Because he was looking for Pooh.

How do we know that Rapunzel liked to party?
Because she was always letting her hair down.

**What was Fireman Sam
called after he retired?**
Sam.

Where does Tarzan buy his clothes?
At a jungle sale.

Who is the best underwater spy?
James Pond.

Food

What do you call two banana skins left on the floor?
A pair of slippers.

Why did the jelly wobble?
Because it saw the milkshake.

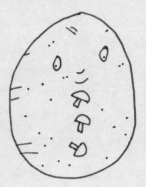

Which vegetable goes best with jacket potatoes?
Button mushrooms.

What would happen if pigs could fly?
Bacon would go up.

How can you make a chicken stew?
Keep it waiting for hours.

What kind of biscuit can fly?
A plane one.

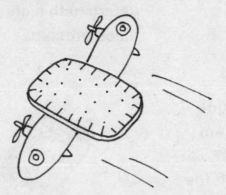

First egg: I don't want to go into the pan of boiling water!
Second egg: It gets worse. When you get out they bash your head in.

Why did the apple cry?
Its peelings were hurt.

What is rhubarb?
*Celery with high
blood pressure.*

**How do you
make a jam
turnover?**
*Push it off the
table.*

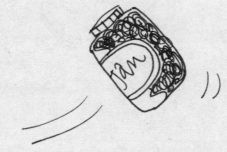

Why is a pancake like a cricket team?
Because they both need a good batter.

What are two things you can't have for breakfast?
Lunch and dinner.

What do you call cheese that doesn't belong to you?
Nacho cheese.

Why don't the French eat two eggs for breakfast?
Because one egg is un oeuf.

**What's orange and
sounds like a parrot?**
A carrot.

**Why shouldn't
you tell an egg
a good joke?**
It might crack up.

What did the tin say to the tin opener?
You make me flip my lid!

How do you make an apple puff?

Chase it round the garden.

What did the toaster say to the loaf?

Pop up and see me sometime.

How do we know that carrots are good for your eyesight?
Well, have you ever seen a rabbit wearing glasses?

What sits in custard looking miserable?
Apple grumble.

What did the egg say to the mixer?
I know when I'm beaten.

Why did the farmer plough his field with a steamroller?
Because he wanted to grow mashed potatoes.

What cheese is made backwards?
Edam.

How do you make a sausage roll?
Push it down a hill.

Laura: There's a lot of juice in this grapefruit.
Chris: Yes, there's more than meets the eye.

Why did the biscuit go to the hospital?
He felt crumby.

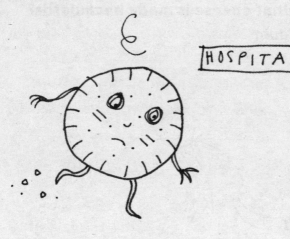

HOSPITAL→

What can a whole orange do that half an orange can't?
Look round.

**What happened when the red
sauce chased the brown sauce?**
It couldn't ketchup.

How do you tease fruit?
Banananananananana!

Why did the tomato blush?
It saw the salad dressing.

Why did the raisin go out with the prune?
Because she couldn't find a date.

Why did Edward stare at the orange juice for two hours?
Because it said 'concentrate'.

Why did the mushroom go to the party?
Because he was a fun guy.

Have you heard the butter joke?
Don't spread it.

What do you get when two strawberries meet?
A strawberry shake.

Why did the banana go to the doctor?
Because it wasn't peeling very well.

**Why did the priest like
Swiss cheese?**
Because it was hole-y.

Why are sausages rude?
*Because they spit when
you fry them.*

Why do the French eat snails? *Because they don't like fast food.*

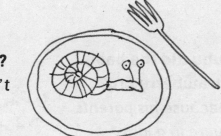

What happens when you sit on a grape? *It gives a little whine.*

How do you make a strawberry shake? *Take it to see a scary movie.*

**Why did the baby
strawberry cry?**
*Because his parents
were in a jam.*

**What's brown, hairy and
wears sunglasses?**
A coconut on holiday.

**Why did the orange stop rolling
down the hill?**
Because it ran out of juice.

**Why can't you tell a secret
in a vegetable garden?**
*The corn has ears and the
potatoes have eyes.*

Why are eggs overrated?
Because they're not all they're cracked up to be.

Where do hamburgers box?
At an onion ring.

What do cornflakes wear on their feet?
Kelloggs.

**How do you make a
banana split?**
Cut it in half.

**What did the mayonnaise
say to the fridge?**
Shut the door, I'm dressing!

Geography

What do you call the small rivers that run into the Nile?
Juveniles.

What is the capital of England?
E.

How do we know that Earth won't come to an end?
Because it's round.

**Which capital city
cheats at exams?**
Peking.

Where would you find Oslo?
On a map.

**In which city can you just
wander round aimlessly?**
Rome.

Which country has the thinnest people?
Finland.

In which country are you most likely to slip and fall?
Greece.

What's the coldest place in the world?
Chile.

Which country suffers from aches?
Spain.

What makes the Tower of Pisa lean?
It doesn't eat much.

What's the best thing to take to the desert?
A thirst-aid kit.

What did the ground say to the earthquake?
You crack me up!

What's in the middle of Paris?
The letter R.

How do you find out what the weather's like at the top of a mountain?
You climate.

Where did the bad choir go on holiday?
Singapore.

Why is the Mississippi such an unusual river?
It has four eyes and can't even see!

What country in Europe satisfies Hungary?
Turkey.

What should you say when the Statue of Liberty sneezes?
God bless America!

Ghosts

What happens when a ghost gets lost in the fog?
He is mist.

What's a baby ghost's favourite game?
Peek-a-boo.

Who sailed the phantom ship?
A skeleton crew.

How did the glamorous ghost earn a living?
She was a cover ghoul.

Where does a ghost train stop?
At a manifestation.

What are pupils at ghost schools called?
Ghoulboys and ghoulgirls.

**What did the young ghost
call his mum and dad?**
Transparents.

How does a ghost make a milkshake?
*He creeps up behind a glass of milk
and shouts, 'Boo!'*

**What kind of ghosts haunt
operating theatres?**
Surgical spirits.

When do ghosts play tricks on each other?
April Ghoul's Day.

What do you get if you cross a ghost with a packet of crisps?
Snacks that go crunch in the night.

What happened when the boy ghost met the girl ghost?
It was love at first fright.

What's a ghost's favourite country?
Wails.

Why don't skeletons jog?
They can't stand the noise.

What's a ghost's favourite tree?
A ceme-tree.

What kind of jewels do ghosts wear?
Tombstones.

Which streets do ghosts haunt?
Dead ends.

How do worried ghosts look?
Grave.

Why are ghosts so bad at lying?
You can see right through them.

What do ghosts like on their roast beef?
Grave-y.

What game do ghosts play at parties?
Haunt and seek.

First ghost: You seem depressed. What's up?
Second ghost: I don't seem to frighten people any more.
First ghost: Tell me about it. We may as well be alive for all they care.

What's a skeleton's favourite song?
Shake, rattle and roll.

Why are graveyards so noisy?
Because of all the coffin.

Why did the skeleton go to the barbecue?
He needed some spare ribs.

**The ghost teacher was talking to her class.
'Now, children, did you understand that?'
she asked. 'If not, watch the board and I'll
go through it again.'**

Why didn't the skeleton ask the other skeleton to dance?
He didn't have the guts.

How do you get a ghost to lie completely flat?
Use a spirit level.

What did the mummy ghost say to her son?
Spook when you're spooken to.

What kind of ghost has the best hearing?
The eeriest.

Why couldn't the ghost stand up?
He had no visible means of support.

What do you call a play acted by ghosts?
A phantomime.

**What kind of music
do ghosts like?**
Haunting melodies.

**Where do ghosts go on
holiday?**
The Dead Sea.

How do we know ghosts are cowards?
Because they haven't got the guts.

Gross!

What vegetable
can you find in
a toilet?
A leek.

Why can't you hear a
pterodactyl go to the toilet?
Because it has a silent P.

How do you cope with a gas leak?
Tell the person to leave the room and
open all the windows.

Why was the nose tired?
Because it never stopped running.

Why did the toilet paper roll down the hill?
Because it wanted to get to the bottom.

What happened to the boy who drank eight cans of cola?
He brought 7 up.

What has four legs, a tail and flies?
A dead horse.

What's invisible and smells like carrots?
Bunny farts.

What's brown and sounds like a bell?
Dung.

Why was the stable boy so busy?
Because his work kept piling up.

History

Why did Henry VIII have so many wives?
He liked to chop and change.

Why did knights in armour practise a lot?
To stop them getting rusty.

What was Camelot famous for?
Its knight life.

**What do you get if you cross
the Atlantic with the *Titanic*?**
Halfway.

**What did the damsel in distress
say to the knight?**
Don't just sit there, slay something!

Why is history fruity?
Because it's full of dates.

Why does history keep repeating itself?
Because nobody was listening the first time.

**Why couldn't cavemen
send birthday cards?**
*The stamps wouldn't
stick to the rocks.*

**Which civilization invented
the fountain pen?**
The Incas.

**What was the speed limit
in ancient Egypt?**
Forty Niles an hour.

**What did the dragon say when he
met a knight in shining armour?**
I love tinned food.

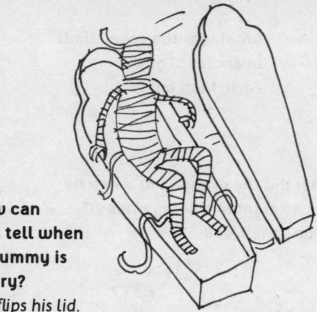

**How can
you tell when
a mummy is
angry?**
He flips his lid.

**How do we know that Rome
was built in a night?**
*Because history tells us it
wasn't built in a day.*

**How did Vikings communicate
with each other?**
Using Norse code.

How do mummies begin their emails?
Tomb it may concern.

How was the Roman Empire divided?
With a pair of Caesars.

Who was the fastest runner in history?
Adam – he was first in the human race.

Caesar: What's the weather like?
Brutus: Hail, Caesar.

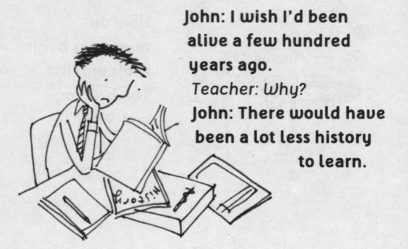

**John: I wish I'd been
alive a few hundred
years ago.**
Teacher: Why?
**John: There would have
been a lot less history
to learn.**

**How do you use an Ancient
Egyptian doorbell?**
Toot and come in.

Why did mummies go on holiday?
To unwind.

**Which monarchs aren't buried
in Westminster Abbey?**
The ones that are still alive.

Why did Robin Hood only rob the rich?
Because the poor didn't have anything worth stealing.

What happened to Lady Godiva's horse when he realized she wasn't wearing any clothes?
It made him shy.

Why are mummies so good at keeping secrets?
Because they keep everything under wraps.

Where was Henry VIII crowned?
On his head.

Who invented fire?
Some bright spark.

Holiday Time

Natalie: I got very badly sunburned on holiday.
Andy: Well, I guess you
basked for it.

**How do you cut
through waves?**
With a sea-saw.

Russell: What did you do in Austria?
*Sam: I thought about going skiing
but then I let it slide.*

Why did the crab blush?
Because the seaweed.

**Hotel guest: Hmmm. This
room's OK, but I'd like
one with a shower.**
*Hotel manager: This isn't
your room, it's the lift.*

Rob: What was your hotel like?

Rachel: Amazing. It had three swimming pools!

Rob: Three?

Rachel: Yep – one full of hot water, one cold water and one empty.

Rob: What use was the empty pool?

Rachel: It was for people who couldn't swim.

Hotel guest: Are the rooms here quiet?
*Hotel manager: Yes, very. It's the guests
who are noisy.*

**Hotel guest: What's your
weekly rate?**
*Hotel receptionist: I don't
know – nobody's ever
stayed that long.*

**Hotel guest: I'd like a room with
a sea view, please.**
*Hotel receptionist:
That's £40 extra per
night.*
**Hotel guest: How
much if I promise
not to look?**

What's yellow, white and travels at 500 miles per hour?
A pilot's egg sandwich.

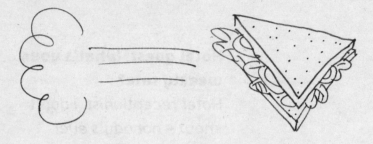

Hotel receptionist: This is the third time you've called – what's eating you?
Hotel guest: That's what I'd like to know!

Ticket inspector: I'm sorry, sir, this train ticket is for London and this train's going to Oxford.
Passenger: Oh dear! Does the driver know he's going the wrong way?

Hotel guest: Do the stairs take you up to the top floor?
Hotel receptionist: I'm afraid not. You'll have to walk.

Rachel: How was your week skiing?
Eddie: Interesting. I spent one day skiing and six in hospital.

Passenger: I'd like a return ticket, please.
Booking clerk: Where to?
Passenger: Back here, of course!

When would you be glad to be down and out?
After a bumpy flight.

A man was hanging over the rail of a cruise ship as it tossed on the waves. A passing steward asked if he was all right.

'No,' replied the man. 'I feel terrible. What shall I do?'

'You'll soon find out,' replied the steward.

British tourist in the USA: Waiter, what's the difference between the $5 steak and the $10 steak?

Waiter: Five dollars.

**What did one rock pool
say to the other?**
Show us your mussels.

**Laura: Can
we take a ladder
on holiday with us?**
Rob: Why?
**Laura: Dad says we're going to do some
climbing.**

Felicity: We're going on a ferry on our holiday.
Emma: Every time I go on a ferry, it makes me cross.

Mum: Why are you writing that postcard so slowly?
*Amy: It's for nan.
She's a slow reader.*

Emily: Do you have trouble deciding where to go on your holidays?
Claire: Well, yes and no.

Chris: You should get a job at the met office.
Jamie: Why?
Chris: Because you're an expert on passing wind.

Mark: You remind me of a film star.
Kate: Who? Scarlett Johansson?
Mark: No, Jaws.

I'll never forget the first time we met, but I'll keep trying anyway.

When people first meet you, they don't like you. But when they get to know you better . . . they hate you.

Matt: You remind me of a Greek statue.
Claire: You mean you think I'm beautiful?
Matt: No – you're not all there.

Lisa: You have the face of a saint.
Oliver: How kind! Which one?
Lisa: Saint Bernard.

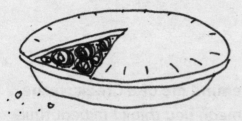

Paul: You remind me of my favourite pie.
Ruth: You mean because I'm all sweetness and light?
Paul: No, because you are a bit crusty.

Sarah: You remind me of the *Mona Lisa*.
Margaret: Because I'm beautiful and have an enigmatic smile?
Sarah: No, because you're old enough to be in a museum.

Laura: I think you're a peach.
Louise: Is that because you think I'm sweet?
Laura: No, because you have a heart of stone.

I'm not saying I find you annoying, but you could give a headache to an aspirin.

You're as strong as an ox, and almost as intelligent.

Listening to you is like the waves of the sea – it makes me sick.

Are you always this stupid or are you just making a special effort today?

I bet your brain feels good as new, seeing as you've never used it.

John: If frozen water is iced water, what is frozen ink?
David: Iced ink.
John: I know you do.

Jobs

Fliss: What does your boyfriend do for a living?
Tracey: He's a pig farmer.
Fliss: Ah, I thought he had a certain air about him.

How do undertakers talk?
In a grave manner.

What did the painter say to the wall?

One more crack like that and I'll plaster you!

**Mark: I'm starting a new job
as a human cannonball.**

Dave: I bet you get fired.

What's the difference between a soldier and a policeman?
You can't dip a policeman in your boiled egg.

Why do surgeons wear masks?
So that if they make a mistake, nobody will know who did it.

What do you call a judge with no thumbs?
Justice Fingers.

**Why did the pilot
land his plane on top
of the house?**
*Because the
landing lights
were on.*

**Why did the secretary have
her fingers cut off?**
So she could do shorthand.

What kind of fish do fishermen catch at night?
Starfish.

Why did the plumber lose his job?
Because it went down the drain.

How did the psychic predict what his friend was getting for his birthday?
He felt his presents.

**What does an executioner
do with a pen and paper?**
Writes his chopping list.

**How do you become a
professor?**
By degrees.

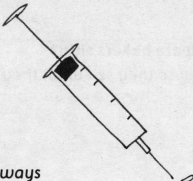

**Why are doctors
like boxers?**
*Because they're always
jabbing people.*

Where do police officers live?

999 Letsby Avenue.

Why are bakers silly?

Because they sell what they knead.

Where do generals keep their armies?

Up their sleevies.

What kind of trees do plumbers prefer?
Toiletries.

What happens when the Queen burps?
She issues a royal pardon.

Circus owner: What was the name of the man who used to put his hand in the lion's mouth?
Tim: I don't know what it used to be, but we call him 'Lefty' now.

What do hangmen read?

Noosepapers.

Why did John go into the bakery business?

Because he wanted to make some dough.

What did the policeman say to his stomach?

Don't move, you're under a vest.

Why did the sword swallower only swallow half the sword?

He was having a mid-knife crisis.

Why did the tap dancer retire?

He kept falling in the sink.

**Which month do
soldiers hate?**
The month of March.

Why are train drivers anxious?
Because their jobs are always on the line.

**Why was thunder and lightning
coming from the laboratory?**
*Because the scientists were
brainstorming.*

How did the farmer mend the holes in his trousers?
With cabbage patches.

Why are cooks cruel?
Because they batter fish and beat eggs.

What kind of training do you need to become a waste collector?
None – you just pick it up as you go along.

How does the man in the moon cut his hair?
Eclipse it.

What is an archaeologist?

Someone whose career is in ruins.

What did the judge say to the dentist?

Do you swear to pull the tooth, the whole tooth and nothing but the tooth?

**What kind of jokes
does a chiropodist
like best?**
Corny ones.

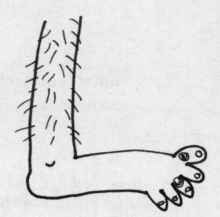

**Why did the sword swallower
swallow an umbrella?**
*He wanted to put something
away for a rainy day.*

**Who earns a living by driving
his customers away?**
A taxi driver.

What does a dentist call his X-rays?
Tooth-pics.

**What kind of shoes
do spies wear?**
Sneakers.

**Why did the farmer plough his
field with a steamroller?**
*Because he wanted to grow
mashed potatoes.*

What happened to the useless woodcutter?

He was axed.

Why are hairdressers such good drivers?

Because they know all the short cuts.

What do you call a vicar on a motorbike?

Rev.

Knock, Knock

Knock, knock
Who's there?
Boo.
Boo who?
Don't cry, it's only a joke.

Knock, knock.
Who's there?
Ice cream.
Ice cream who?
Ice cream if you don't let me in!

Knock, knock.
Who's there?
Justin.
Justin who?
Justin time for dinner!

Knock, knock.
Who's there?
Lettuce.
Lettuce who?
Lettuce in and we'll tell you!

Knock, knock.
Who's there?
Dan.
Dan who?
Dan druff.

Knock, knock.
Who's there?
Bella.
Bella who?
Bella not working, that's why I knocka.

Knock, knock.
Who's there?
Honeycomb.
Honeycomb who?
Honeycomb your hair!

Knock, knock.
Who's there?
Europe.
Europe who?
Europe early this morning!

Knock, knock.
Who's there?
Luke.
Luke who?
Luke through the spyhole and you'll find out!

Knock, knock.
Who's there?
Francis.
Francis who?
Francis a country in Europe.

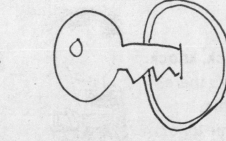

Knock, knock.
Who's there?
Mikey.
Mikey who?
Mikey is stuck in the keyhole!

Knock, knock.
Who's there?
Interrupting cow.
Interru—
MOO MOOOOOO MOO MOOOOOOOO MOO!

Knock, knock.
Who's there?
Major.
Major who?
Major open the door!

Knock, knock.
Who's there?
Archie.
Archie who?
Bless you!

Knock, knock.
Who's there?
Howard.
Howard who?
Howard I know?

Knock, knock.
Who's there?
Armageddon.
Armageddon who?
Armageddon outta here!

Knock, knock.
Who's there?
Amos.
Amos who?
Amos-quito bit me!

Knock, knock.
Who's there?
Cash.
Cash who?
No thanks, I'm allergic to nuts.

Knock, knock.
Who's there?
Canoe.
Canoe who?
Canoe come out to play?

Love

Edward: Will you still love me when I'm old and grey?
Annie: Of course I do.

Dan: How could I ever leave you?
Felicity: By bus, train, car, plane . . .

Simon: What would it take for you to kiss me?
Laura: Anaesthetic.

Luke received an email from his ex-girlfriend.
'Dear Luke,' it read. 'I'm so sorry I called you ugly and said I never wanted to see you again. I've had time to think it over and I'd even marry you if you wanted me to. Please email me back. Love Rachel. PS Congratulations on winning the lottery.

Husband: Did you miss me while I was away?
Wife: Have you been away?

Tom: Could you be happy with a boy like me?
Amelia: Maybe. As long as he wasn't too much like you.

Magic

What happens to witches who get in trouble at magic school?
They get ex-spelled.

Why is English a witch's best subject?
Because she's so good at spelling.

What kind of jewellery do witches wear?
Charm bracelets.

What should you give an elf who wants to be taller?
Elf-raising flower.

Why do witches fly on broomsticks?
Because vacuum-cleaner cords aren't long enough.

What do you call a nervous witch?
A twitch.

Why did the witch lose her voice?
She had a frog in her throat.

**How do you make a
witch scratch?**
Take away the W.

**What do you get when you cross a
witch with an ice cube?**
A cold spell.

What do elves do after school?
Gnomework.

What kind of witch likes cheese and ham?
A sandwich.

What happens when a witch loses her temper?
She flies off the handle.

Monsters

Why did the
one-eyed
monster have
to close his
school?
*He only had one
pupil.*

Why did the monster buy a hammer?
To burst his pimples.

**Which monster
makes strange
noises in its
throat?**
The gargoyle.

**What did the werewolf
say to his victims?**
It's been nice gnawing you.

On which day do monsters eat people?
Chewsday.

Why do dragons sleep during the day?
So they can fight knights.

Why did the monster get good marks in his exam?
Because two heads are better than one.

**Why did the monster slice
the top of his head off?**
*Because he wanted to keep
an open mind.*

How do monsters count to thirteen?
On their fingers.

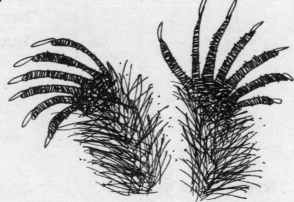

**Why did the Cyclops apply
for half a TV licence?**
Because he only had one eye.

What do you call a monster in a phone box?
Stuck.

How did the yeti feel when he caught the flu?
Abominable.

First zombie: You look tired.
Second zombie: Yes, I'm dead on my feet.

**What do you call a werewolf who
sleeps with the windows open?**
A fresh-air fiend.

**How does Frankenstein
eat his dinner?**
He bolts it down.

**What do monsters
make with cars?**
Traffic jam.

What do you do with a blue monster?
Try to cheer him up.

What's a monster's favourite ballet?
Swamp lake.

First monster: Am I late for dinner?
Second monster: Yes. Everybody's been eaten.

**Why do monsters forget
everything you tell them?**
*Because it goes in one ear
and out the others.*

How do monsters like their shepherd's pie?
Made with real shepherds.

What kind of monster lives in your nose?
A bogeyman.

**What will a
monster eat in a
restaurant?**
The waiter.

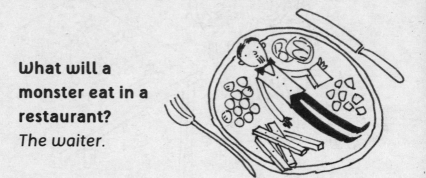

**How does a
monster greet a
human?**
Pleased to eat you.

What do sea monsters eat?
Fish and ships.

**First monster: That girl just
rolled her eyes at me!**
*Second monster: Well, roll them
back, she might need them later.*

Why did the monster give up boxing?
He didn't want to spoil his looks.

Music

How did the guitarist leave the band?
On a sour note.

What do you get when you drop a piano on an army base?
A flat major.

Why do bagpipers walk when they play?
To get away from the noise.

What do you get if you drop a piano down a mine shaft?
A flat minor.

Why did the orchestra have bad manners?
Because it didn't know how to conduct itself.

Why did the composer spend all his time in bed?
He wrote sheet music.

Did you hear about the violinist who was in tune?
Neither did I.

What did the guitar say to the guitarist?
Pick on someone your own size.

Why is it difficult to open a piano?
Because all the keys are inside.

Why was the musician arrested?
Because he got into treble.

Why are pianos so noble?
Because they're either upright or grand.

Piano tuner: I've come to tune the piano.
Pianist: But we didn't call you.
Piano tuner: No, but your neighbour did.

Why didn't the musical instruments email each other?
They preferred to write notes.

Which musical instrument can be used to catch fish?
A castanet.

Nature

**What did the big flower
say to the little flower?**
What's up, bud?

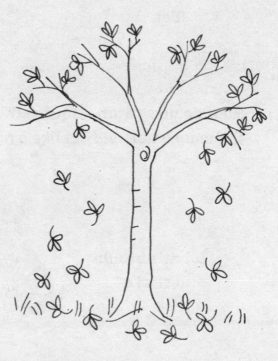

**What does a
tree do when
he's ready to
go home?**
He leaves.

**What do you get when you cross
a river with a stream?**
Wet.

How do you catch a squirrel?
Climb up a tree and act like a nut.

**What's brown
and sticky?**
A stick.

How can you tell that the ocean is friendly?
It waves.

What did the beaver say to the tree?
It's been nice gnawing you.

Why was the insect thrown out of the forest?
Because he was a litter bug.

What lies at the bottom of the ocean and shakes?
A nervous wreck.

Why did the tide turn?
Because the seaweed.

Why is a river rich?

Because it has two banks.

Laura: I've just touched some nettles.

Chris: That was rash.

What do sad fir trees do?
Pine.

Why do toadstools grow close together?
They don't need mushroom.

What washes up on tiny beaches?
Micro waves.

What kind of tree is good at maths?
A geo-me-tree.

Claire: What's green, dangerous and grows in fields?

Natasha: I don't know.

Claire: Grass.

Natasha: But why is it dangerous?

Claire: Because it's full of blades.

Pirates

What's a pirate's favourite school subject?
Aaaart.

Why couldn't the pirate play cards?
Because he was sitting on the deck.

Why are pirates called pirates?
Because they aaaaarrrrr!

Why are pirate flags always in a bad mood?
Because they have crossbones.

What did the pirate name his daughter?
Peggy.

How much do pirates pay for their earrings?
A buccaneer.

Why does it take a pirate so long to learn the alphabet?
Because they can spend years at C.

Whose parrot said 'Pieces of four, pieces of four'?
Short John Silver.

School

Why did the music teacher need a ladder?
So she could reach the high notes.

Joanne: I really don't think I deserve a zero for this test.
Teacher: Neither do I, but it's the lowest mark I can give you.

What time is it when you sit on a drawing pin?
Spring time.

Head teacher: You missed school yesterday, didn't you, Jamie?
Jamie: Not even slightly.

What do you call a teacher wearing headphones?
Anything you like, he can't hear you!

Mum: Oh my goodness! Why have you got a black eye?
Matt: I hammered a thumb in woodwork class.
Mum: But that doesn't explain the black eye.
Matt: It wasn't my thumb.

Why was the head teacher worried?
*Because there were so many rulers
in the school.*

Why is school like a shower?
*One wrong turn and you'll find
yourself in hot water.*

Why did the teacher wear sunglasses?
Because her pupils were so bright.

Teacher: Name two days of the week that begin with T.
Pupil: Today and Tomorrow.

When can school uniforms be fire hazards?
When they are blazers.

Teacher: How many books have you read in your lifetime?
Pupil: I don't know yet, I'm still alive!

Teacher: Name five things that you might see at the zoo.
Claire: A tiger . . . and four monkeys.

What do you get if you cross your least favourite teacher with a telescope?
A horrorscope.

Why were the teacher's eyes crossed?
Because she couldn't control her pupils.

Teacher: What can you tell me about Queen Victoria?
Anna: She's dead.

Teacher: Matt, define 'artery'.
Matt: The study of paintings.

Why was the maths book sad?
Because it had too many problems.

Lauren: Dad, can you write in the dark?

Dad: I can have a go – what do you want me to write?

Lauren: Your signature on my report card.

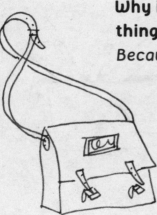

Why is a pencil the heaviest thing in your school bag?

Because it's made of lead.

Teacher: Why is your exam paper blank, Emma?

Emma: I used invisible ink.

How do teachers dress in winter?
Quickly.

Teacher: What do you get if you multiply 3,684 by 20?
Steph: The wrong answer.

At school I had a fear of the hundred-metre hurdles, but I got over it.

Teacher: Who was the Roman Queen of the Gods?

Sarah: Juno.

Teacher: I do, but I'm asking you.

Cookery teacher: You must be very careful in the kitchen, Liam. Most accidents at home happen in the kitchen.

*Liam: *sighs*
I know, and I usually have to eat them.*

My teacher doesn't know ANYTHING. All she does is ask questions.

Teacher: What does 'coincidence' mean?
Chris: That's funny, I was going to ask you the same thing.

Did you hear about the maths teacher who fainted in class?
Her pupils tried to bring her 2.

**When is a blue school book
not a blue school book?**
When it's read.

**What's the best thing
about being a teacher?**
August.

Teacher: Who can tell me the difference between like and love?
Jenny: Well, I like my mum, but I LOVE my new shoes.

Dad: How are your marks at school, Ben?
Ben: They're underwater.
Dad: What?
Ben: They're below C.

Teacher: I hope I didn't see you looking at Kate's paper.
Adam: I hope you didn't either.

What did the bookworm say to the school librarian?
Please can I burrow this book?

I would tell you
the joke about
the blunt pencil,
but it's pointless.

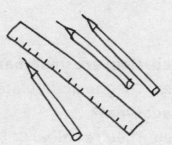

Teacher: If you had five chocolate bars, and your little brother asked you for one, how many would you have left?
Rachel: Five.

Why did the student eat his homework?
The teacher told him it was a piece of cake.

Why should a school not be near a chicken farm?
So the children don't overhear any fowl language.

What's an inkling?
A baby fountain pen.

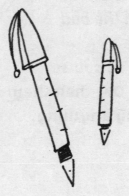

Chris: Would you punish someone for something they hadn't done?
Teacher: Of course not.
Chris: Good, because I haven't done my homework.

Teacher: What did your parents say about your report card?
Edward: Shall I leave out the bad language?
Teacher: Of course.
Edward: OK, then they didn't say anything.

Did you hear about the brilliant geography teacher?
He had abroad knowledge of his subject.

Teacher: Today we'll be learning about percentages. If you take a test of ten questions, and you answer them all correctly, what do you get?
Pupil: Accused of cheating.

Pupil: Miss, how do you spell 'ississippi'?
Teacher: Do you mean 'Mississippi'?
Pupil: No, I've written the M already.

Science and Technology

What did one magnet say to the other magnet?
I find you very attractive.

What did the hungry computer say?
I could go for a byte.

Which travels faster: heat or cold?
Heat – you can catch a cold.

**What did one earthquake
say to the other
earthquake?**
It's not my fault.

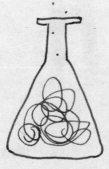

**Why did the germ cross
the microscope?**
To get to the other slide.

What happens if you eat uranium?
You get atomic-ache.

What animal do you have inside your computer?
RAM.

Teacher: What's HNO$_3$?
Chris: Er, um, ah . . . it's on the tip of my tongue . . .
Teacher: Then you'd better spit it out quickly – it's nitric acid!

What happened when the wheel was invented?
It caused a revolution.

Why was the computer cold?
It left its windows open.

Archimedes: Eureka!
Mrs Archimedes: Yes, you don't smell too good yourself.

What happens if you get a gigabyte?
It megahertz.

Emma: When I die I'm going to leave my brain to science.
Jamie: Well, I suppose every little bit helps.

What is the centre of gravity?
The letter V.

What is H_2O_4?
To drink.

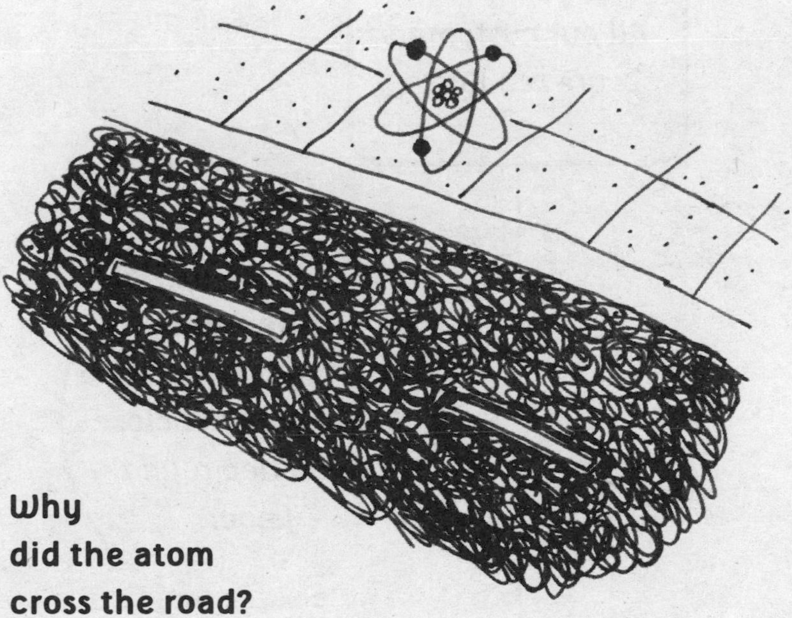

**Why
did the atom
cross the road?**
It was time to split.

Silly Signs

Genuine, strong, hot curries.
All our customers are regular.

Order your ring by post!
State size or enclose string tied round finger.

NOTICE IN MEN'S TOILETS:

We aim to keep these
toilets clean at all times.
Your aim will help.

SIGN IN DELICATESSEN:

Our
tongue
sandwiches
speak for
themselves.

**SIGN ON WALL OF
PUBLIC TOILET:**

In the interest
of economy
please use both
sides of the
toilet paper.

SIGN IN CAFE:

> Don't complain
> about the tea.
> You might be
> old and weak
> yourself one day.

SIGN IN LAUNDERETTE:

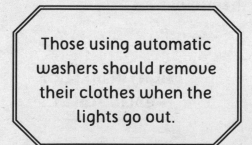

> Those using automatic
> washers should remove
> their clothes when the
> lights go out.

Space

How do you get a baby
astronaut to sleep?
You rock-et.

Why did the scientist
disconnect his doorbell?
*He wanted to win the
Nobel prize.*

What did Mars say to Saturn?

Give me a ring some time.

What did the astronaut see in the frying pan?
An unidentified frying object.

Why don't astronauts get hungry after being blasted into space?
Because they've just had a big launch.

Why was the alien such a good gardener?
Because he had green fingers.

**How does a Martian know
when he's attractive?**
When bits of metal stick to him.

**Where do
Martians go
for a drink?**
Mars bars.

What's a spaceman's favourite game?
Astronauts and crosses.

Where do aliens leave their flying saucers?
At parking meteors.

Which is heavier: a full moon or a half moon?
A half moon, because a full moon is lighter.

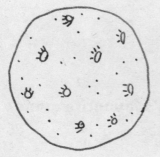

**How did the solar
system keep its trousers up?**
With an asteroid belt.

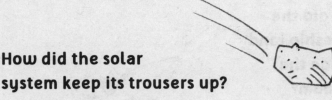

What holds the moon up in the sky?
Moonbeams.

**What did E.T.'s parents say to
him when he got home?**
Where on earth have you been?

**Why did the
spaceship land
outside the
bedroom?**
*Someone had left the
landing light on.*

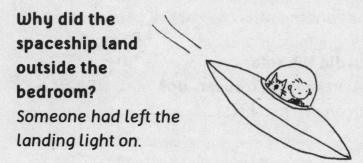

Why did the Martian go to the optician?
He had stars in his eyes.

Why did the alien wear a bulletproof vest?
Because of all the shooting stars.

**What do you call a
wizard from outer space?**
A flying sorcerer.

What did the alien say to the gardener?
Take me to your weeder.

**What did one shooting star
say to the other?**
Pleased to meteor!

Where do aliens keep their sandwiches?
In a launch box.

Sport

Why did the football quit the team?
It was tired of being kicked around.

What tea do footballers drink?
Penal-tea.

What's the hardest thing about learning to ride a horse?
The ground.

How can you keep cool at a football match?
Stand next to a fan.

How did the football pitch become a triangle?
Someone took a corner.

Did you hear about the time Mark tried to swim across the lake?
When he was halfway to the other side he decided he was too tired to carry on, so he turned round and swam back again.

Why can't two waiters play tennis?
They only want to serve.

Why do bicycles fall over?
Because they're two tyred.

Why did the chicken get sent off?
For fowl play.

**How can you swim a mile
in just a few seconds?**
Go over a waterfall.

Kate: What are you doing on Saturday?
Steve: Watching United play.
**Kate: Wow. Do you get really excited
when they win?**
*Steve: I'm not sure. I've only been going
for two seasons.*

How long does it take to learn to ice skate?
A hundred sittings.

Why did the cricket team hire a cook?
They needed a good batter.

Coach: Twenty teams in the league and you finish bottom!
Captain: Well, it could have been worse.
Coach: How?
Captain: There could have been more teams in the league.

What's the very lowest sport you can play?
Baseball.

Why are fish rubbish at tennis?
Because they don't like getting close to the net.

Emma: What happened to you?
Rachel: I fell while I was riding.
Emma: Horseback?
Rachel: I don't know, I'll find out when I get back to the stables.

Which athlete is never promoted?
The left back.

When is cricket a crime?
When there's a hit and run.

What did the baseball glove say to the baseball?
Catch you later.

What happens to a footballer when his eyesight starts to fail?
He becomes a referee.

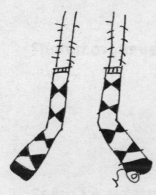

Why did the golfer carry an extra pair of socks?
In case he got a hole in one.

**Which athlete stays
the warmest?**
The long jumper.

What do athletes eat for lunch?
Runner beans.

**Why do footballers carry
handkerchiefs?**
Because they're always dribbling.

Vampires

Where did the vampire keep his valuables?
In a blood bank.

Why was Dracula sad?
He loved in vein.

What do vampires take before going to bed?
A bloodbath.

Why did the vampire's wife leave him?
He was a pain in the neck.

Why are vampires like false teeth?
Because they come out at night.

What happened when the boy vampire met the girl vampire?
It was love at first bite.

What's as sharp as a vampire's fang?
His other fang.

**What comes out at night, and
goes bite, bite, OUCH?**
A vampire with toothache.

Are vampires mad?
Well, they're often bats.

Why did the vampire take an art class?
Because he liked to draw blood.

Why do vampires always travel with their coffins?
Because their lives are at stake.

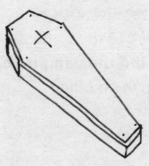

What do you call a short vampire?
A pain in the leg.

What do you get if you cross a vampire with a plumber?
A bloodbath.

Why did the vampire become an actor?
It was in his blood.

Why did the vampire buy a red pen?
So he could draw blood.

What do baby vampires say at bedtime?
Read me a gory!

What does a tired vampire do?
Takes a coffin break.

What's the best way to talk to a vampire?
On the phone.

**What's a vampire's
favourite fruit?**
A neck-tarine.

What day do vampires hate?
Sun-day.

Why don't vampires ever get fat?
Because they eat necks to nothing.

What kind of ship does Dracula have?
A blood vessel.

What's a vampire's favourite soup?
Scream of tomato.

Little vampire: Mummy, am I definitely a vampire?
Mummy vampire: Yes, dear.
Little vampire: Are you sure?
Mummy vampire: Yes, dear, positive. Why do you ask?
Little vampire: Because whenever I see blood, I faint.

Mummy, what's a vampire?
Shh, darling. Eat your soup before it clots.

Waiter!

Waiter, I simply can't eat this food.
Please get me the manager.
He won't eat it either, sir.

Waiter, please be careful!
Your thumb is in my soup!
Not to worry, madam, it isn't very hot.

Waiter, why on earth is there
a footprint on my pie?
You did ask me to step on it, sir.

Waiter, this egg is bad.
Don't blame me, sir, I only laid the table.

**Waiter, bring me something to eat,
and make it snappy.**
How about a crocodile sandwich, madam?

Waiter, do you serve fish?
Of course, sir, we'll serve anyone.

**Waiter, this coffee
tastes like mud.**
*That doesn't
surprise me, it was
ground only a few
moments ago.*

Waiter, these eggs taste funny.
Then laugh, sir.

Waiter, there appears to be a dead beetle in my water.
Yes, sir, they aren't very good swimmers.

Waiter, do you have frogs' legs?
No, sir, it's just the way I walk.

**Waiter, what on earth
is that fly doing on
my ice cream?**
Learning to ski, sir.

How did you find your steak, sir?
Well, I just moved a chip and there it was.

Waiter, will my omelette be long?
No, madam, it will be round.

Waiter, my plate's all wet!
That's your soup, sir.

Waiter, I've just seen a caterpillar in my lettuce!
Don't worry, madam, we won't charge you any extra.

Waiter, is there spaghetti on the menu?
Yes, let me get a cloth to wipe it off.

Weather

Why do hurricanes travel so fast?
Because if they didn't, we'd have
to call them slowicanes.

**Why isn't the sky happy on
clear days?**
Because it has
the blues.

**What did one lightning bolt
say to the other lightning bolt?**
You're shocking!

What did one snowman say to the other snowman?
Can you smell carrots?

What do you call a lovely warm sunny day following two rainy days?
Monday.

What do clouds wear under their clothes?
Thunderwear.

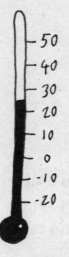

How do hurricanes see?
With one eye.

How do you catch a snowman?
Hide behind a bush and make a noise like a carrot.

Why is lightning badly behaved?
Because it doesn't know how to conduct itself.

What is wind?
Air in a hurry.

What did one cloud say to the other?
I'm cirrus about you.

What kind of music do lightning bolts listen to?
Rock 'n' roll.

What is a volcano?
A mountain with hiccups.

What do you call . . .

What do you call a man with a toilet on his head?
John.

What do you call a woman with two toilets on her head?
Lulu.

What do you call a man on your doorstep?
Mat.

What do you call a woman who stands astride a river?
Bridget.

What do you call a man with no legs?
Neil.

What do you call a woman with a weight on one side of her head?
Eileen.

What do you call a man on your doormat?
Bill.

What do you call a girl with a frog on her head?
Lily.

What do you call a man with gravy, meat and potatoes on his head?
Stew.

**What do you call a man
in a pile of leaves?**
Russell.

**What do you call a man with
a rabbit up his jumper?**
Warren.

**What do you call a man with a
car number plate on his head?**
Reg.

**What do you call a man with
a spade on his head?**
Doug.

**What do you call a man without
a spade on his head?**
Douglas.

**What do you call a man
with a seagull on his head?**
Cliff.

**What do you call a man with a
bag of compost on his head?**
Pete.

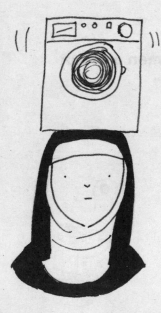

**What do you call a
nun with a washing
machine on her head?**
Sister Matic.

**What do you call a woman with
a cash register on her head?**
Tilly.

**What do you call a woman
with slates on her head?**
Ruth.

**What do you call a woman
with a tortoise on her head?**
Shelley.

**What do you call a fish
with no eyes?**
A fsh.

What do you call a man with a car on his head?

Jack.

What do you call a man who likes to dunk biscuits in his tea?

Duncan.

What do you call a man with a cow on his head?

Pat.

What do you call
a woman who
slides around on
a piece of hot
toast?
Marge.

What do you call a deer with no eyes?
No idea.

What do you call a deer
with no eyes and no legs?
Still no idea.

**What do you call a man
floating in a swimming pool?**
Bob.

**What do you call a woman
with a storm on her head?**
Gail.

**What do you call a man with a large
black and blue mark on his head?**
Bruce.

What do you call a camel without a hump?
Humphrey.

What do you call a cow with two legs?
Lean beef.

What do you call a cow with no legs?
Ground beef.

?

BUM-BELIEVABLE!

A fabulous bumper book of facts containing everything you ever wanted to know about sport, medicine, space, ghosts, inventions, monarchs throughout history, vampires, dinosaurs and much, much more!
It's bum-believable!

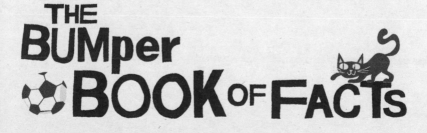

THE BUMper BOOK OF FACTs

SUPER GEEK!

DINOSAURS, BRAINS & SUPERTRAINS

GLENN MURPHY

THE WORLD CANNOT SURVIVE WITHOUT THE WISDOM OF
THE QUICK-WITTED GEEK. HOW MUCH DO *YOU*
REALLY KNOW ABOUT THE SCIENCE THAT MATTERS?

WHAT KIND OF ANIMAL WAS A *MEGALODON*?
HOW LONG COULD YOU SURVIVE WITH ONLY *HALF* A BRAIN?
HOW LARGE WOULD AN ASTEROID HAVE TO BE TO
WIPE OUT ALL HUMAN LIFE ON THE PLANET?

FIND OUT THE ANSWERS TO THESE AND AN AWFUL LOT OF
OTHER BRILLIANT QUESTIONS IN THIS BRAIN-BOGGLING QUIZ
BOOK WHICH WILL TEST THE BRAINIEST OF SUPERGEEKS.
ARE YOU GEEK ENOUGH?

GLENN MURPHY, AUTHOR OF WHY IS SNOT GREEN?, SETS THE
QUESTIONS AND GIVES THE ANSWERS IN THIS FUN-FILLED
BOOK OF CHALLENGES WITH NO BORING BITS!

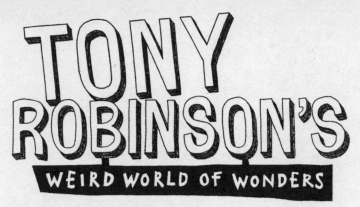

TONY ROBINSON'S
WEIRD WORLD OF WONDERS

Hello, we're the Curiosity Crew. You'll probably spot us hanging about in these books checking stuff out.

Jojo

Stig

Peewee

Grace

Nits

TONY ROBINSON'S
WEIRD WORLD OF WONDERS
ROMANS

TONY ROBINSON'S
WEIRD WORLD OF WONDERS
EGYPTIANS

TONY ROBINSON'S
WEIRD WORLD OF WONDERS
INVENTIONS

TONY ROBINSON'S
WEIRD WORLD OF WONDERS
BRITISH

TONY ROBINSON'S
WEIRD WORLD OF WONDERS
WORLD WAR II

TONY ROBINSON'S
WEIRD WORLD OF WONDERS
GREEKS